SINCE 2021

A is for Ancient

Sharks have been swimming

in the ocean for a very,

very long time, even before

dinosaurs!

AAAAAAAAAAAAAAAAAAAAAAAAAA

aaaaaaaaaaaaaaaaaaaaaaaaaaaa

A is also for Awesome:

Sharks are awesome

because they come in

many sizes and colors,

just like our toys!

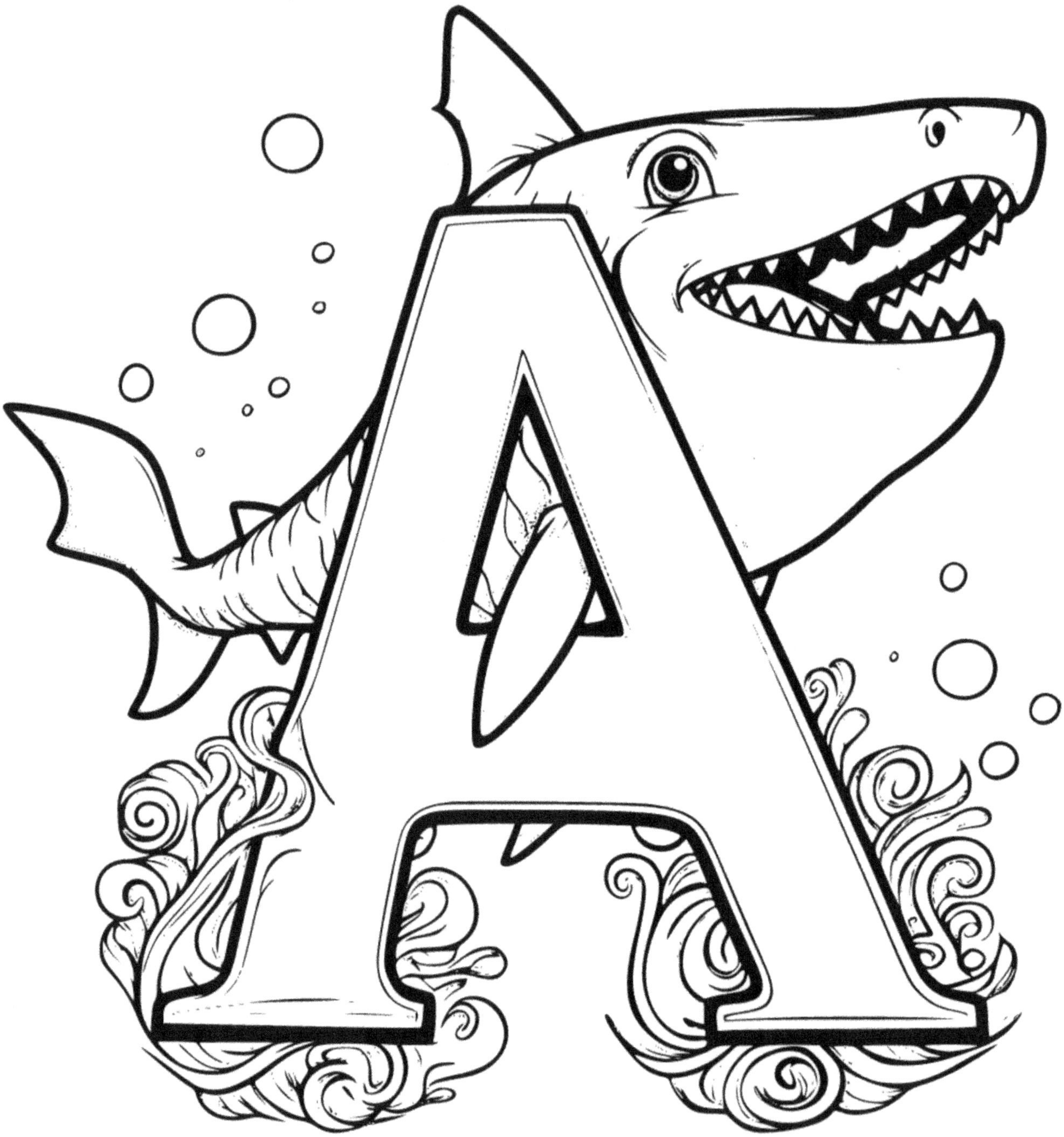

A A A A A A A A A A A A A A A A A A

a a a a a a a a a a a a a a a a a a a a a a

B is for Bones.

Sharks don't have

bones inside them, they

have squishy cartilage,

like our nose and ears.

B is also for Big.

Some sharks can grow

as big as a school bus,

and some are as small

as our pet goldfish!

C is for Colors.

Sharks can be gray,

blue, or even spotted like

a ladybug. They're like a

rainbow in the sea!

CCCCCCCCCCCCCCCCCCCC

CCCCCCCCCCCCCCCCCCCCCCC

C is also for Curious.

Sharks are curious about

what's in the water, and

they explore their ocean

home.

CCCCCCCCCCCCCCCCCCC

CCCCCCCCCCCCCCCCCCCCCC

D is for Dance.

Sharks need to keep

swimming all the time to

breathe, so they dance

underwater like ballerinas!

D is also for Dangerous.

But don't worry, most sharks

are not dangerous to us

because they have more

important things to do in the

sea.

DDDDDDDDDDDDDDDDDD

ddddddddddddddddddddddddddddddd

E is for Eyes.

Sharks have big, bright
eyes that help them see
in the dark ocean
waters.

E is also for Eating.

They have many sharp

teeth and love to eat

yummy fish and other

sea creatures.

F is for Fast

Some sharks can swim

super fast, faster than

a race car in the

water!

F is also for Fin.

Sharks have special

fins, like airplane wings,

that help them glide

through the ocean.

G is for Gills.

Sharks use their gills

to breathe underwater,

like how we use our

lungs to breathe air.

G is also for Gentle.

Some sharks are

very gentle, just like

our pets at home.

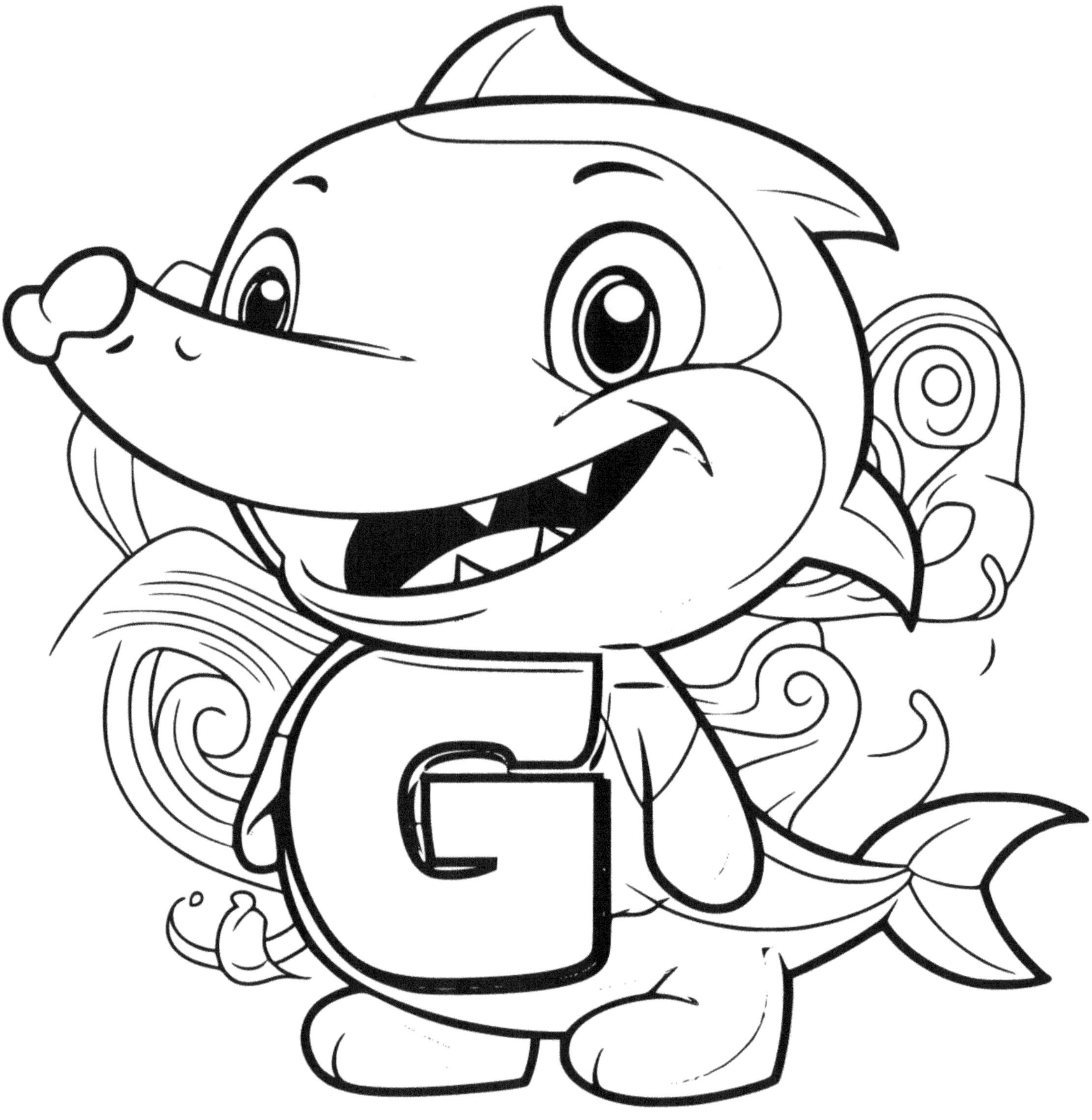

GGGGGGGGGGGGGGGGGG

gggggggggggggggggggggg

H is for Hunt.

Sharks hunt for food

by using their great

sense of smell to find

tasty treats.

H is also for Hammerhead.

The hammerhead shark

has a head that looks like

a hammer, which is funny

and cool

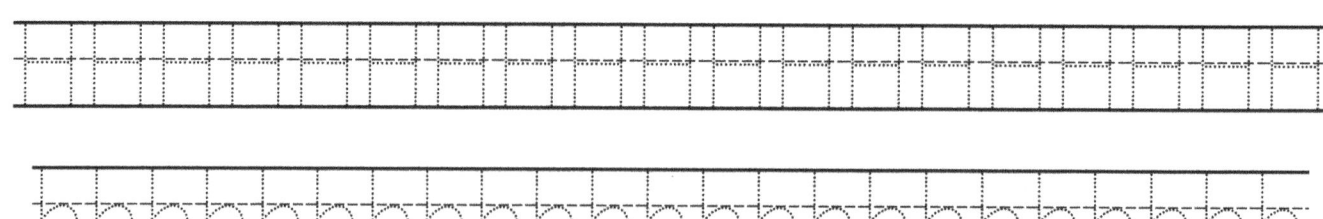

I is for Incredible.

Sharks are incredible

creatures, and we can

learn so much about

them.

I is also for Important.

Sharks are important to

the ocean because they

help keep it clean and

healthy.

J is for Jaws.

Sharks have strong

jaws with sharp teeth,

like a superhero's

secret weapon!

J J J J J J J J J J J J J J J J J

j j j j j j j j j j j j j j j j j j j j j j j j j j j j j j j j j j j j j j j j j j j j j j j j

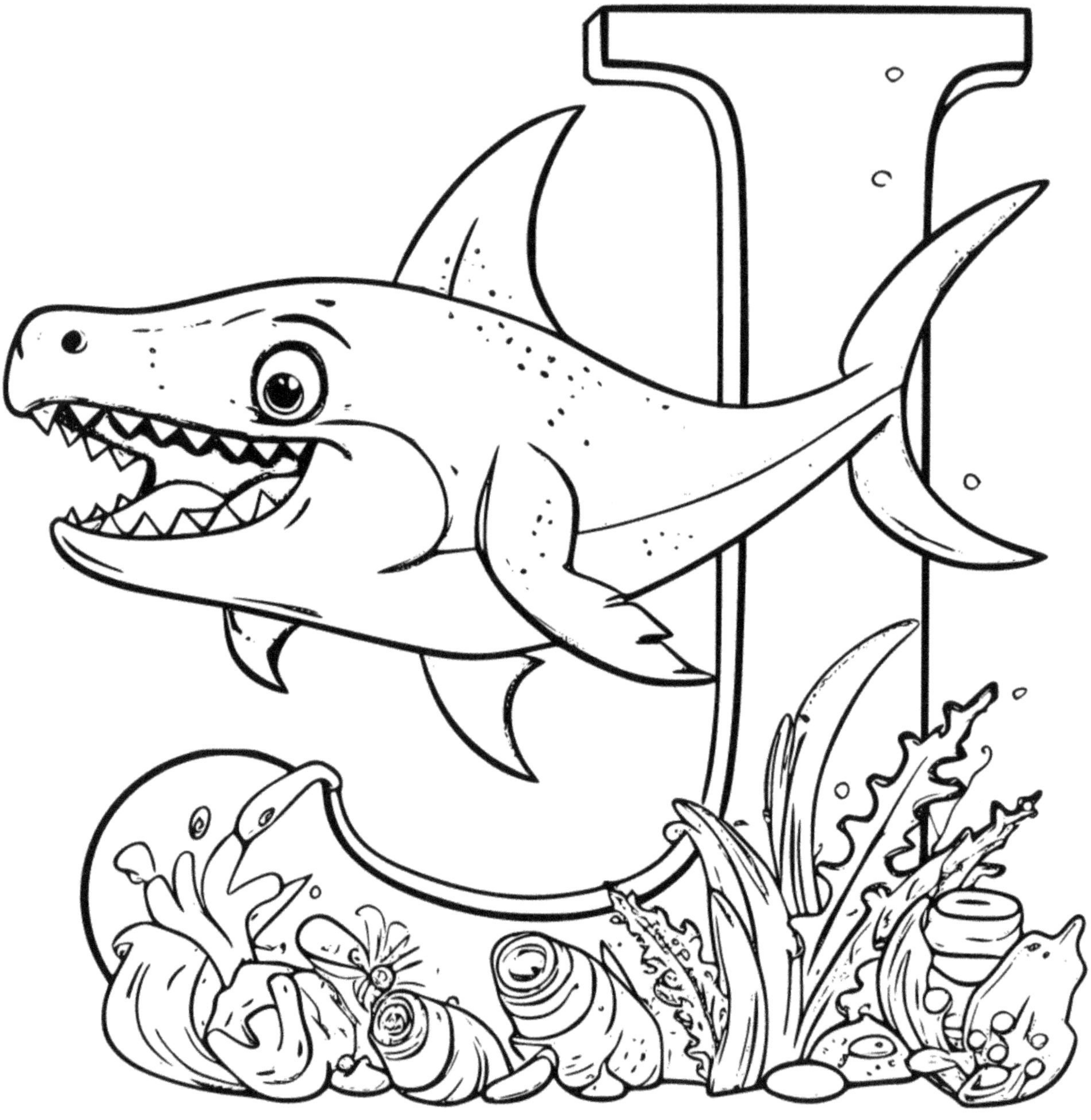

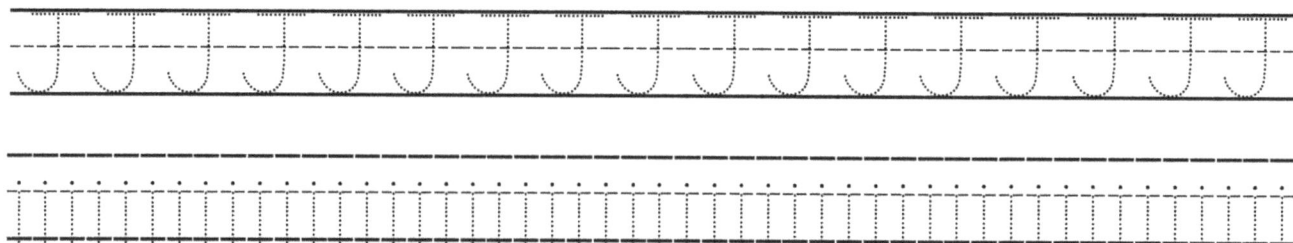

J is also for Jump.

Some sharks can jump

out of the water, like

dolphins, to say hello to

the sky.

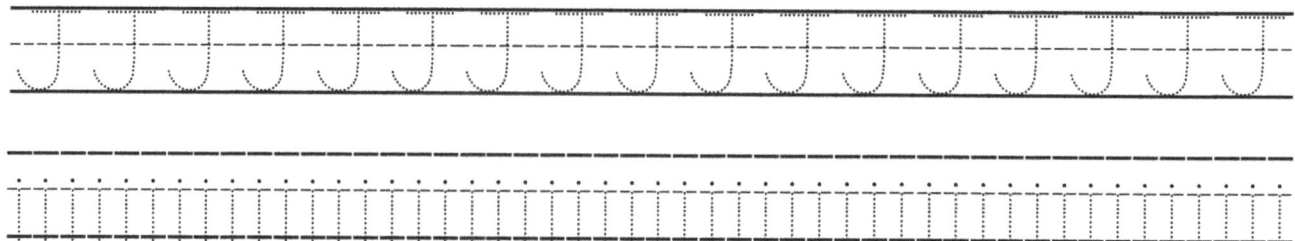

K is for Kids.

Even little kids like

us can learn about

and love sharks!

KKKKKKKKKKKKKKKKK

KKKKKKKKKKKKKKKKK

K is also for Kind.

Sharks are kind to

the ocean by eating

old or sick animals.

L is for little.

Some sharks are as

little as our toys,

like baby sharks!

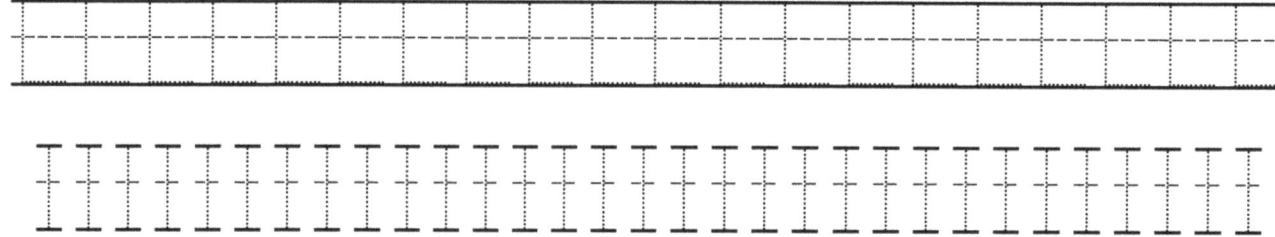

L is also for Large.

Others are as large as

big trucks, and they

can be super long.

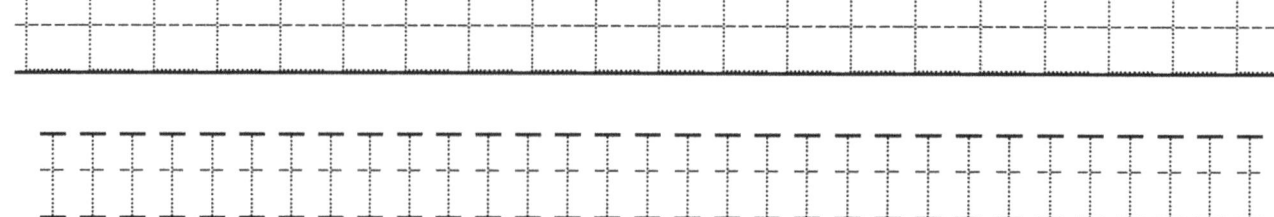

M is for Music.

Sharks don't make

music, but their

movements in the water

are like a special

underwater dance!

M is also for Mysterious.

The deep sea, where

sharks live, is mysterious

and full of secrets.

MMMMMMMMMMMMMMM

mmmmmmmmmmmmmm

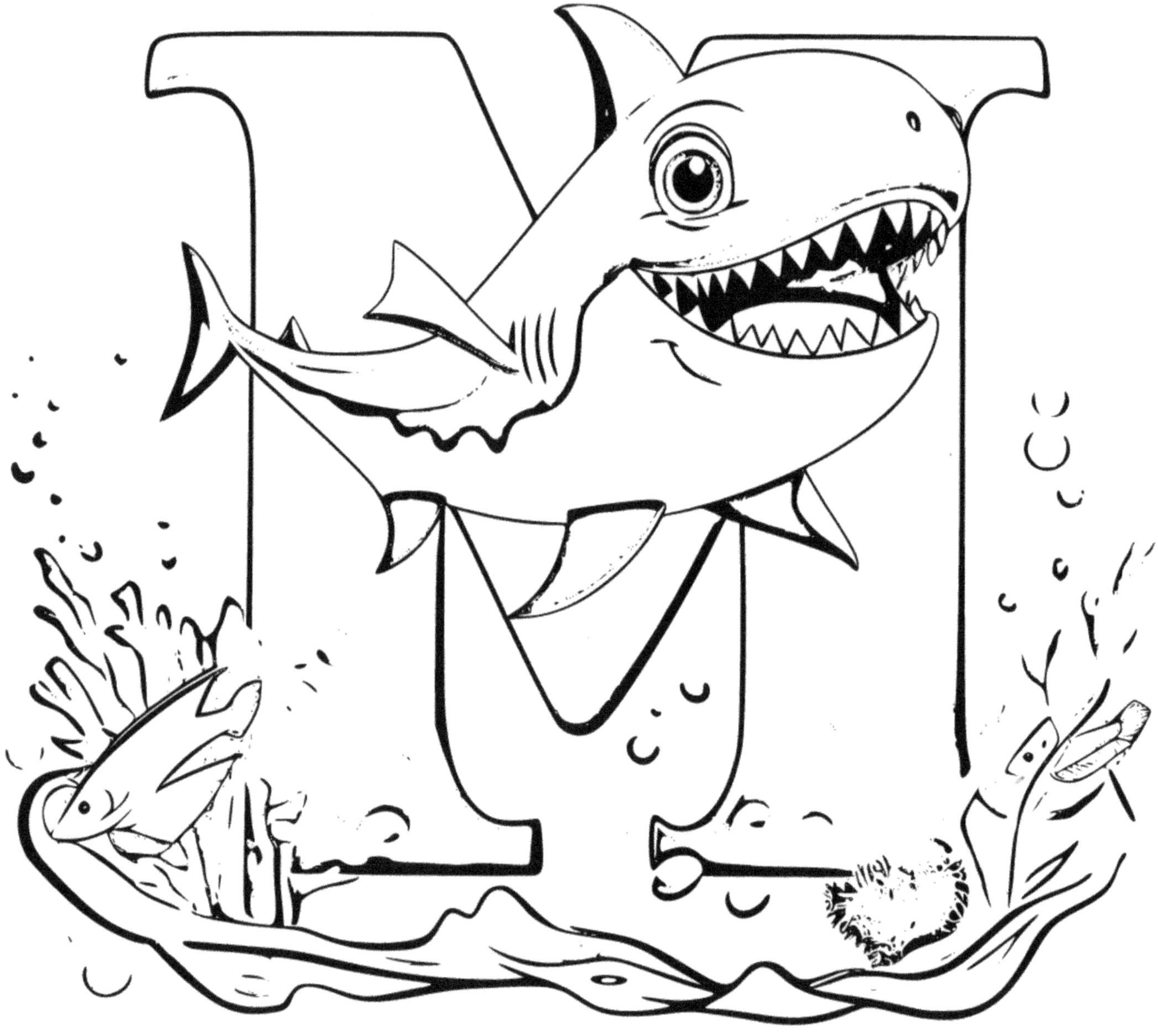

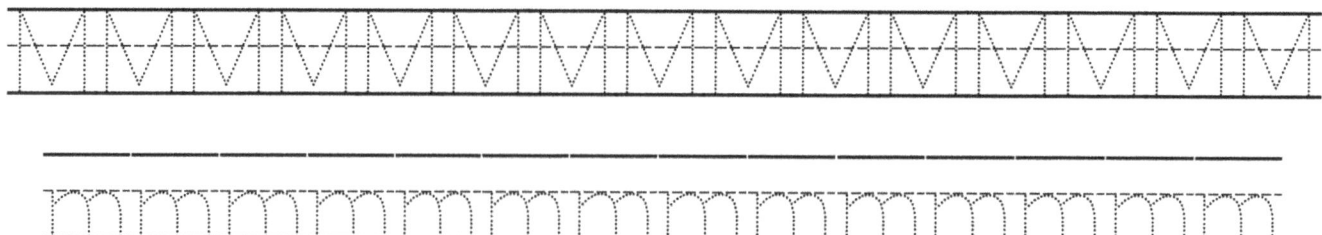

N is for Nostrils.

Sharks use their nostrils
to smell food, even if it's
very far away, like a
superhero's superpower!

N is also for Night.

Some sharks like to

swim at night when it's

dark, like a bedtime

adventure.

O is for Ocean.

Sharks live in the big,

blue ocean, which is their

home, just like our house

is our home.

O is also for

Oceanography. That's a big

word, but it means

scientists study the ocean

and all its amazing

creatures, like sharks.

P is for Pectoral Fins.

Sharks have special fins

that help them steer and

balance in the water, like

the wings on an airplane!

PPPPPPPPPPPPPPPPPPPPP

pppppppppppppppppppp

P is also for Play:
Sometimes, sharks
play by swimming and
leaping in the waves
like we do at the
beach.

Q is for Quiet.

Sharks are often quiet
and sneaky when they
search for their food in
the deep sea.

Q is also for Queen.

The ocean is like a

kingdom, and sharks are

the kings and queens of

the underwater world.

R is for Rough Skin.

A shark's skin feels

rough, like sandpaper,

because it's covered in

tiny, tough scales.

R is also for Roar.
Sharks don't really
roar, but they can
splash and make big
waves.

S is for Size.

Sharks come in many
sizes, from small like
our toys to big like a
school bus.

S is also for Sun.

Sharks like to swim
in the sunshine that
shines through the
water.

T is for Tail.

Sharks use their strong

tails to swim gracefully

through the ocean, like a

superhero's cape!

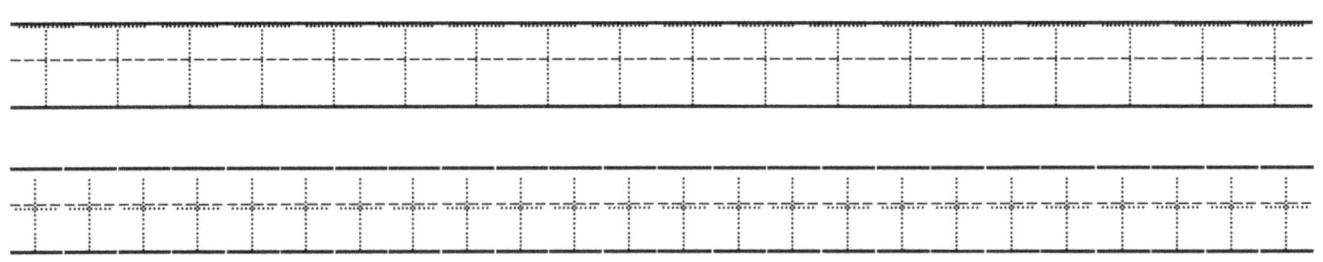

T is also for teeth.

Sharks have lots of

sharp teeth, like little

swords in their

mouths.

U is for Underwater.

Sharks live their whole

lives underwater, and

it's like a big, hidden

world.

U is also for Unique.

Each shark is unique

and special in its way,

just like we are.

Underwater

Alphabets

V is for Variety.
There are many
different types of
sharks, like the many
flavors of ice cream we
enjoy.

V is also for Vacation.
Sometimes, we go on
vacation to the beach
and might see sharks in
the ocean from a safe
distance.

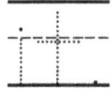

W is for Wonder.

The ocean is full of

wonders, and sharks are

some of the most

fascinating creatures in

it.

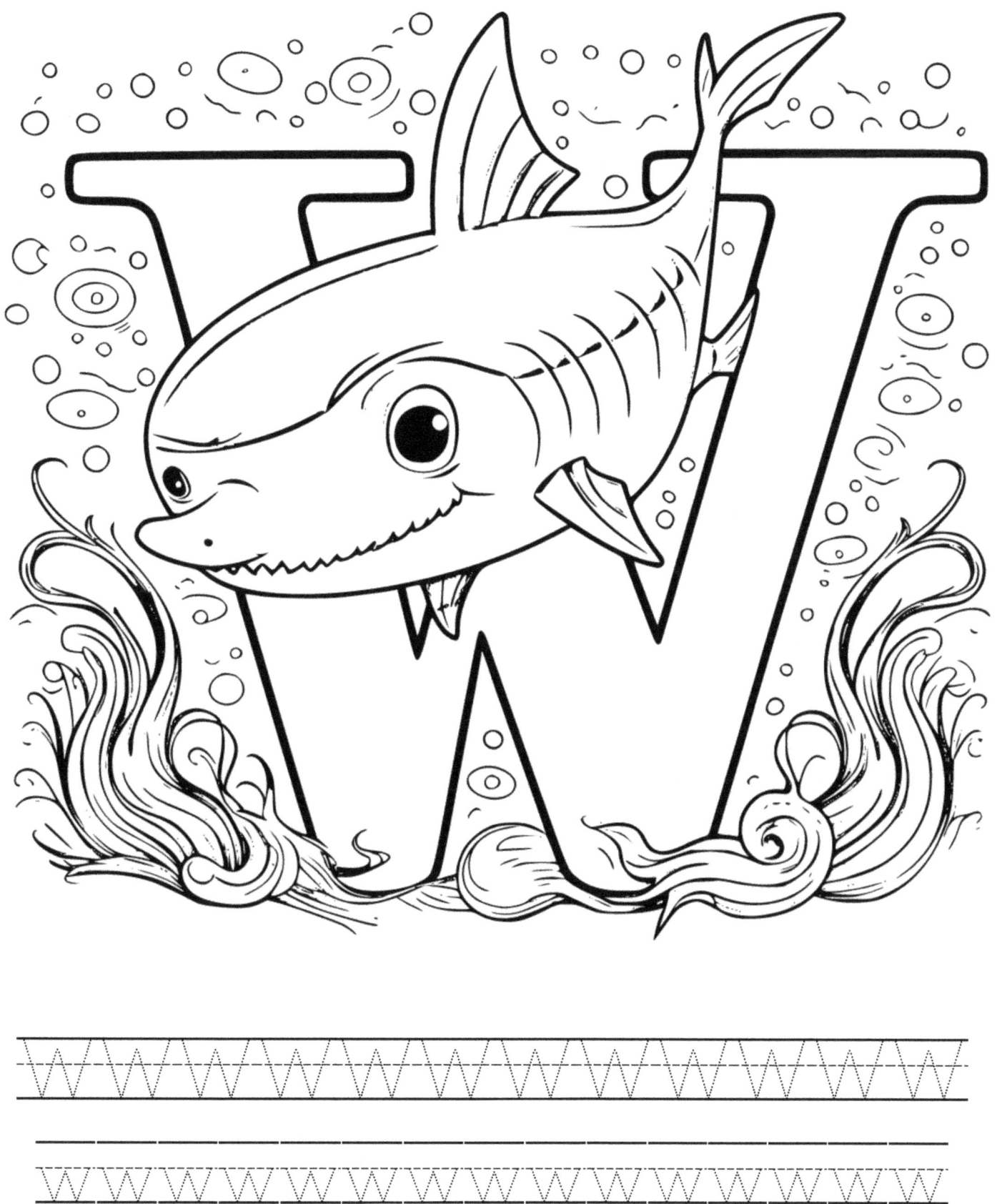

W is also for Water.

Sharks need clean and

healthy water to live,

just like we need clean

air to breathe.

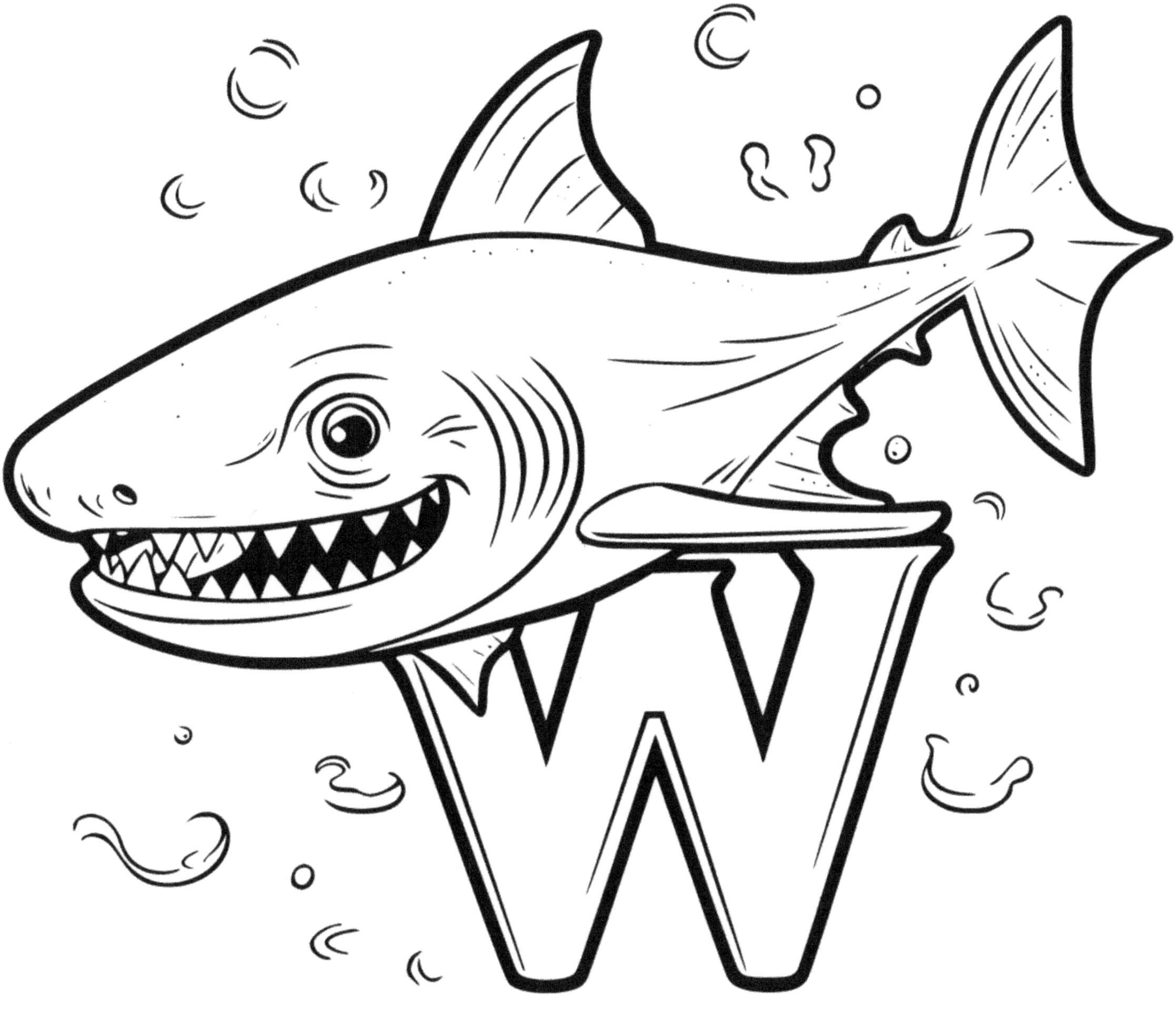

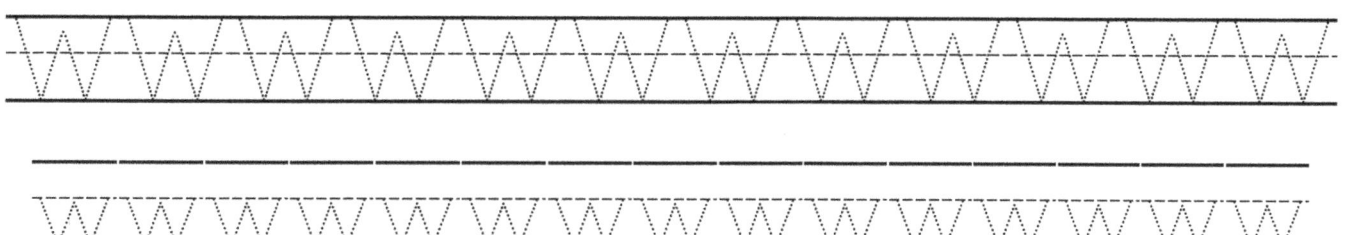

X is for exciting.

Learning about sharks

is an exciting adventure,

like a treasure hunt in

the sea!

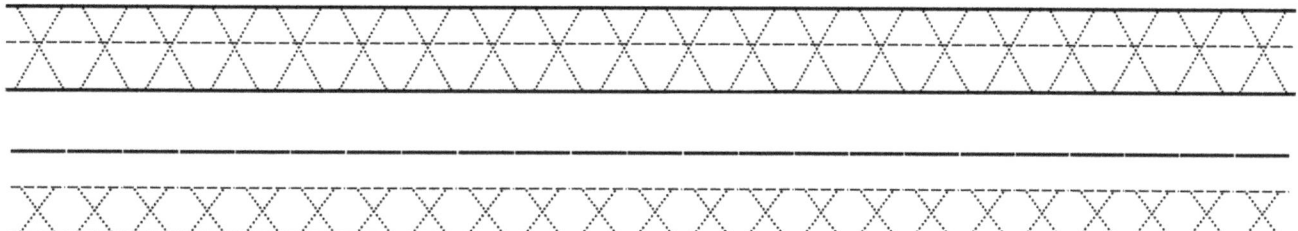

X is also for explore.

We can explore the

world of sharks and

discover new things

about them.

Y is for Yawning.

Sharks don't yawn like
we do, but they open
their mouths wide to
catch their food.

Y Y Y Y Y Y Y Y Y Y Y Y Y Y Y Y Y Y Y Y Y

y y y y y y y y y y y y y y y y y y y y

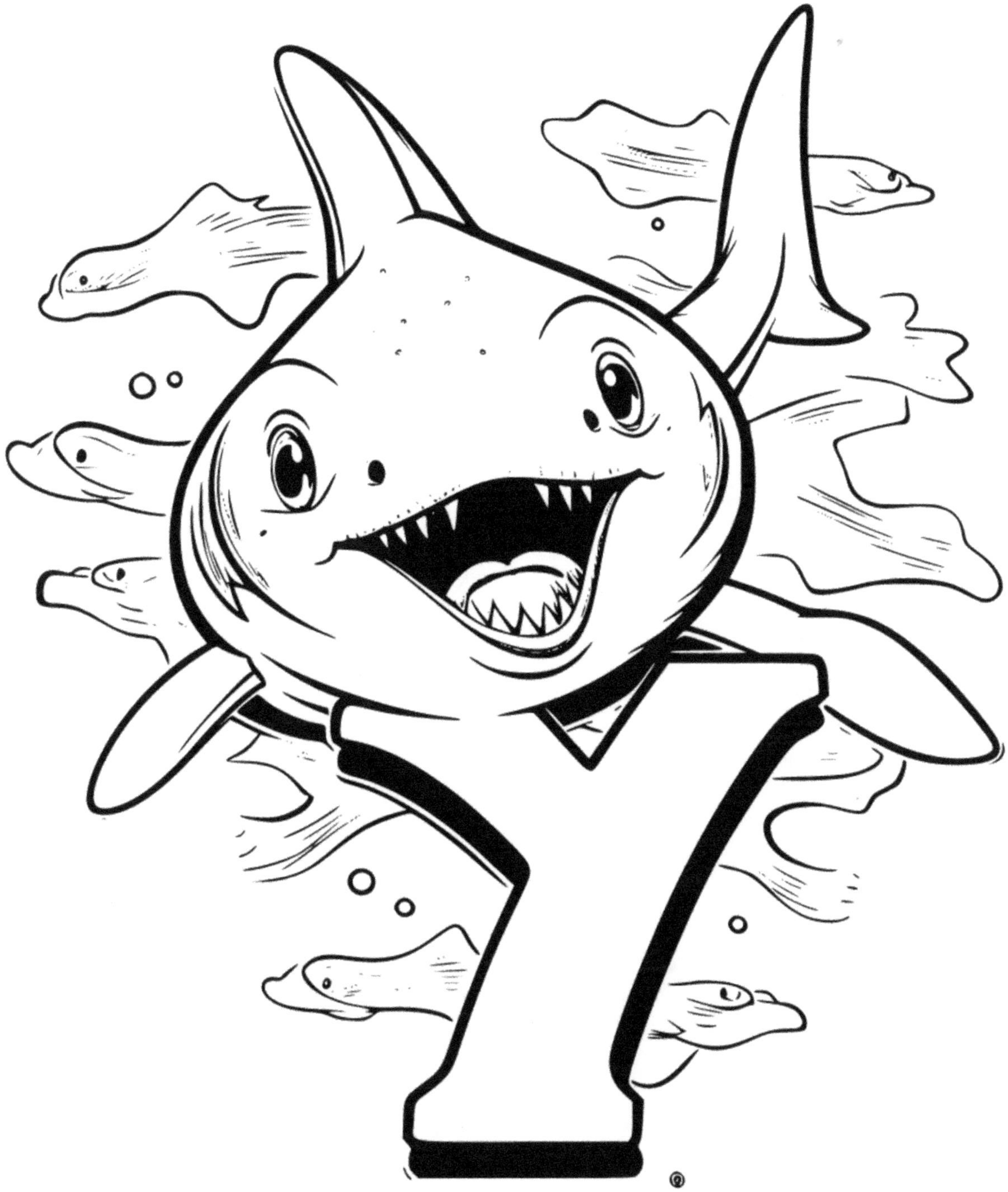

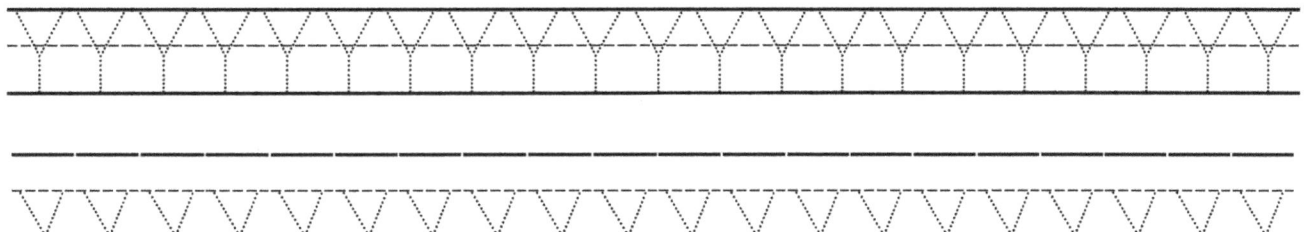

Y is also for Yellow.

Sometimes, the sun

makes the ocean water

look yellow and beautiful.

Z is for Zigzag.

Some sharks move in

zigzag patterns while

they hunt for food, like

racing cars on a track.

Z is also for Zenith.
It's a big word, but it
means that sharks are
at the top of the
underwater food chain,
like kings and queens of
the sea.